SUPERSTARS 78 ANNUAL

CONTENTS

Published in Great Britain by World Distributors (Manchester) Limited,
A Member of the Pentos Group, P.O. Box 111,
12 Lever Street, Manchester M60 1TS.
Printed in Italy.
SBN 7235 0422 9

SUPER SLIK!

SCOTLAND is famous for haggis, the Bay City Rollers and whisky – and for a great new group called Slik.

Exponents of Jockrock (rock music from north of the border) Slik originated in Glasgow. Jim McGinlay (bass) brought the group together by choosing the best members from various local bands, and persuading them to join forces. A group called Salvation was the result, with a line-up of Jim plus Midge Ure (lead vocals and guitar), Billy McIsaac (guitar and piano) and Kenny Hyslop (drums) and the band played around Glasgow for about two years, often sharing the bill with the Bay City Rollers.

Their big chance came when they signed a recording contract with Bell Records, and the boys felt that this change in their fortunes deserved a change in style, too. The boys went out and had their long hair cropped into US college boy style, and added the baseball shirts, narrow trousers and sneakers that have given them such a strong identity with the fans.

They really took off when *Forever and Ever* was released, and since then have collected a strong following all over the country. Slik look set to join that list of Scotland's popular exports. . . .

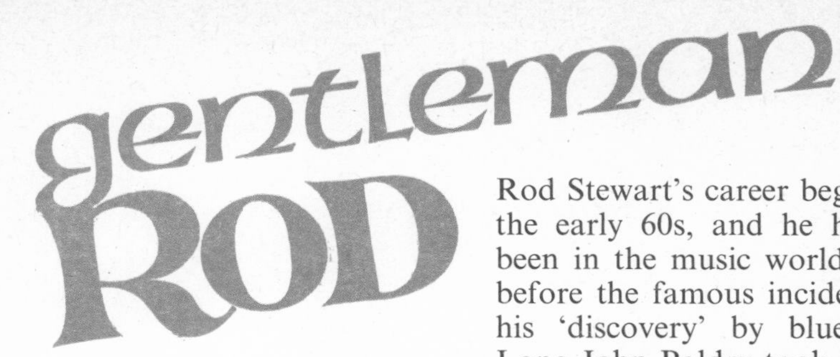

How would you define a superstar? Someone who's been successful for a number of years? Someone who wins praise from the critics as well as the public? Or simply someone with thousands of fans? Whichever of those categories you'd choose, the elegant chap in the boater fits neatly into it. Let's meet . . .

Rod Stewart's career began in the early 60s, and he hadn't been in the music world long before the famous incident of his 'discovery' by bluesman Long John Baldry took place. Just in case you haven't heard the story it's worth telling again.

It seems that young Rod was sitting on the platform of Twickenham railway station, amusing himself by singing odd little snatches of song. Long John listened, liked what he heard, and there and then invited Rod to play a gig with his band, the Hoochie Coochie Men.

That gig went well, and Rod stayed with the band. For the next few years he worked in various bands which were very influential at the time, such as Steampacket, Shotgun Express and The Jeff Beck Group.

The next step, of course, was joining Faces, who were one of the great Supergroups, with every member being a well respected name, and the band as a whole earning a fantastic fan following. Rod Stewart and Faces were hugely successful, with albums like *Every Picture Tells A Story* becoming classic collections of songs for thousands of rock music fans.

It was in December 1975 that Rod announced his decision to leave Faces and move on to other things. His solo album *Atlantic Crossing* and the single from it, *Sailing* were received with delight by his dedicated fans, who had been waiting with interest to see what Rod would come up with next.

All in all, it seems that Rod Stewart really deserves that impressive title: Superstar.

1976 was a very special year for British skating. It was the year that John Curry became European, Olympic and World champion, and brought some self-respect back to British sport.

Success didn't happen overnight for this quietly-spoken man from the Midlands. When he first started to skate his progress was slow, and he would work for weeks and weeks to perfect even simple movements, before moving on to more difficult ones. Ken Vickers, his coach at the Solihull rink, insisted that his basic technique was sound, and John has since had cause to thank him for his good advice.

By the time he reached his teens, John had decided that skating was the life for him, and he moved to London, taking a job as a part-time bank clerk so that he could continue to train. His hard work paid off, and in 1967 he became the British junior champion, although some people criticised his graceful arm and hand movements as being too feminine. But John wanted to make skating less of a sport and more of an art, and he continued to perfect his movements, considering them to be even more important than the athletic jumps and spins.

He continued to work part-time although he was living on the bread line, and he trained for six or seven hours every day, trying to keep out of the way of members of the public as they wobbled round the rink. In 1970 he won the British title, and a year later he began to make a name for himself in Europe too, coming seventh in the European championship.

John had been noticed in America too, and in 1973 Ed Moser, an industrialist, offered to sponsor him. After coming a disappointing fourth in the European championships, John decided that if he was to improve his placing, he would have to go to America to train.

CURRY!

Moser agreed, and at last John had the chance to train in an empty rink. One of his coaches, Carlo Fassi, also trained Dorothy Hammill, who won the gold medal for women's figure skating. She too was sponsored by Ed Moser.

The move across the Atlantic brought results, and in 1975 John was placed second in Europe, behind his greatest rival Vladimir Kovalev of Russia. His career almost ended here, for he complained that the Eastern European judges were biased towards their own competitors. The Soviet Federation asked that he be disqualified, but fortunately this request was refused and the judges were given a discreet warning about biased marking.

John was still being criticised for his arm movements, and he realised that he would have to shift the emphasis back to the jumps and spins if he wanted to reach the top. Another problem was nerves, so Fassi sent him on a two-week course to the Erhard Seminar Training School in New York. Here he learned to conquer the pre-competition nerves so that when he went out onto the ice he was in complete control of himself.

And he needed to be, for he was given the nerve-racking task of skating first in the Olympic final. John skated calmly onto the ice, and it was obvious from the start that he was unbeatable. He gave an impeccable performance, with perfectly executed jumps, axels and spins, as well as a singularly graceful interpretation of the music. His rivals had an impossible task ahead of them, and even the East European judges hadn't the nerve to mark another skater higher. John Curry won the gold medal, becoming only the third Briton ever to win a gold for figure skating.

After winning the three supreme titles in the world, what next? John decided to give up competitive skating. But don't worry . . . this superb talent won't be wasted, for he intends to channel it into the world of entertainment, where it will be appreciated as the art form he has made it.

Cuba's Track King

The emergent athletics nation at the Montreal Olympics was undoubtedly Cuba. From being unknowns and no-hopes as far as international competition was concerned, they came to the fore as a nation to be reckoned with.

The man at the head of the breakthrough into international competition is Alberto Juantorena – the man they call Supersprint, and winner of gold medals in the 400 and 800 metre finals.

Until his wins, Cuba had never before won a gold athletics medal. Tall and imposing, Juantorena first came to notice a couple of years ago when he beat a world-class field (including Britain's David Jenkins) in the World Student Games. But it was at the Olympic Games that he really shook established US track stars, and stormed home for gold in both the 400 and 800 metre finals.

The great upsurge in athletics talent is even more amazing when you realise that facilities on the island are meagre: just one Tartan track. But if facilities are lacking, enthusiasm isn't: no track is left unused, and young athletes wait patiently for their turn to train.

With athletes of the calibre of Alberto Juantorena, Cuba looks set to become a real force to be reckoned with in international athletics.

Below. Alberto Juantorena heads for the tape in the 400m final ahead of Newhouse and Frazier, both of the US.

Above. The man they call *White Lightning* wins the gold!

BIG HEADED?

NOT BARRY!

The story of Barry Sheene's miraculous fight-back from his 175m.p.h. Daytona spill to the World 500c.c. title is familiar to all motor cycle racing fans. The way Barry shrugged off his terrible injuries to lift the crown is a story of bravery and dedication that would make a Hollywood scriptwriter blush.

But that is Barry Sheene: the easy-going Londoner ready to model underpants and after-shave, eager to help maintain motor cycling's growing popularity and keep the smile permanently on his bank manager's face. Barry has managed to win the approval of a star-hungry public while still holding the respect of the hordes of caravan-dwelling owner-riders that make up the backbone of the sport in this country.

Seven times champion Phil Read, whose rise to the top was both long and hard, has nothing but respect for Sheene's skill. Mick Grant, Barry Ditchburn, and John Williams all acknowledge that Barry is a very hard man to beat on evenly-matched machines, and recognise his efforts to keep motor cycling in the public eye. In a competitive and sometimes hostile industry this is no mean feat and takes more than a quick smile and a nice set of leathers.

Barry Sheene's popularity speaks for itself.

Seventeen years ago three brothers from Los Angeles teamed up with a cousin and a friend to record the single *Surfin'*. Now, with getting on for forty best selling albums under their belts the Beach Boys are still going strong, their rich, exciting music as fresh and successful as ever.

The Beach Boys are best known for simple, fun-loving, HAPPY songs and they wouldn't have it any other way. But one of the reasons they have stayed at the top so long is that in Brian Wilson they have a composer of the highest order. Behind the exuberant celebrations of surfing, drag-racing and cruising for burgers are strong, original melodies and amazingly intricate arrangements. The lyrics are careful, humorous and straight to the point, exploring the American way of life with considerable insight and wit.

The technical excellence of the Beach Boys' vocals does not inhibit the energy and imagination of their famous harmonies. There have been hundreds of imitators, but none can match the Beach Boys for sheer class, a fact underlined by the continued success of their *Best of* albums and other compilations of their old hits.

Seventeen years producing some of the finest pop records ever made is an achievement few other groups can match. Seventeen years of joyful music and they're still at it now – to the eternal gratitude of their millions of fans throughout the world.

Meanwhile, still or

Twiggy

Twiggy has had the sort of career every girl dreams of. Discovered at 15 in a hairdressing salon she was whisked into the world of high fashion modelling and became the face of the sixties. At the top of her profession she was offered the lead in Ken Russell's musical film, *The Boyfriend,* playing opposite Christopher Gable.

Having proved that she could sing and dance, Twiggy left modelling behind. She played Cinderella in a London pantomime, appeared first on other people's T.V. shows and then in her own series, and she played her first serious role in one of a series of plays called *Victorian Scandals.*

But what she really wanted to do was sing, and finally, in 1976, she recorded her first album, simply called *Twiggy.* The single taken from it, *Here I Go Again,* reached the top twenty, and the critics had to admit that Twiggy could sing. The skinny little model from London has blossomed into a talented young woman. She has even put on weight, but after ten years as Twiggy, her name is one thing that won't change!

the beach...

Chicago ~ Ten years on

In a rock music world where new bands rise to fame with their first single and two months later are completely forgotten, it's quite something to find a group which has stayed the course for more than five or six years.

Chicago, originally known as Chicago Transit Authority, were formed in 1968, so they're high up in the list of what you might call 'long players'!

For many years they've tended to be an 'albums band', and they've amassed a huge following of fans, some of whom have been loyal since the release of their first album *Chicago* in 1969. That album was received with great acclaim by critics and public alike, and subsequent albums have all been big sellers, and have shown interesting variations and adaptations of the group's style.

With the release of their single *If You Leave Me Now*, however, they found a whole new audience of enthusiastic fans. The single really brought them into the limelight. It was a huge seller, and remained at the top of the charts for many weeks after its release late in 1976.

Chicago use a fascinating range of instruments, and they are always innovative, making exciting new sounds in rock, jazz, mid-tempo blues, and a kind of lyrical, soft music, of which their tremendously successful single is a good example.

Our photo shows vocalist Peter Cetera, who has been with Chicago since its formation, and whose distinctive voice can be heard on *If You Leave Me Now*.

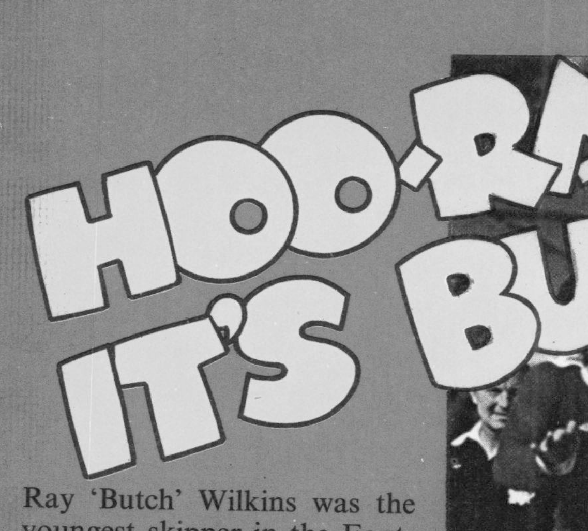

HOO-RAY IT'S BUTCH!

Ray 'Butch' Wilkins was the youngest skipper in the Football League when Eddie McCreadie made him captain of Chelsea during the 1973-4 season. At the end of that season Chelsea were relegated from Division One.

But don't blame Butch. The club was in turmoil when he took the captain's job. The old show-biz styled team had broken up amid a welter of bad-tempered accusations and the club was crippled by the financial burden incurred by the building of their magnificent stand. For a time there was talk of them having to fold.

Butch responded by offering to take a cut in salary, and when Liverpool came in with an offer he said he would rather stay and help Chelsea fight for survival. He was a thrilling example to the many other youngsters that Eddie McCreadie had thrown together in the side.

Their first season in the Second Division was one of consolidation, with the youngsters learning to play together, learning to mould their fast, skilful running and enthusiasm into a cohesive unit. Butch still found the time to turn out for England in the Bi-Centennial tournament in America however, the youngest player for some time to win one of those coveted caps.

As well as being football's number one heart-throb to thousands of girl fans, Butch can play a bit. He is a strong, quick tackler, he reads the game well for someone his age, he can pass a ball with either foot and he's not afraid to have a go should the chance arise. Here he chases a pass to the wing in the match against Bolton.

On the attack. Butch splits the Bolton defence.

The 1976-77 season saw Chelsea really blossom, with Butch showing them the way. Now McCreadie's boys are men and ready to challenge the country's best. Chelsea are back in business and the crowds are coming back. How different it might have been if Butch hadn't stayed.

introducing...

"This is another fine mess you've gotten me into!"

Swimming in the rain!

Starsky and Hutch, the tough, crime-busting duo with the soft centre. Two good-looking cops the fans would love to get under lock and key. Between them they provide action, excitement, and plenty of humour, in what must be the most popular cops-and-robbers series yet. But what about the men behind Starsky and Hutch? Here are a few of the facts on two of the most wanted men around.

David Soul, who plays Hutch, in thoughtful mood.

David Soul, who plays blond, supercool (usually) Hutch, actually began his career as a singer. He called himself 'The Covered Man', and for some strange reason he covered up those good looks with a mask! However, the combination of the mask and a good singing voice intrigued the talent spotter for Columbia TV, Renee Valente, and she decided to take him on.

Under her supervision David studied drama, camera techniques and karate, but it was a few years before the big break came. His first starring role was in a series called *Here Comes the Brides,* and then of course he was offered the part of Hutch, and has never looked back! He hasn't forgotten his music though, and likes to play the piano and guitar in his spare time.

Paul Michael Glaser knew he wanted to act right from the start, and he took his chosen career very seriously. He studied drama at Boston University, and used his holidays to get all the practice he could at a local theatre. After graduating he moved to New York, and there he gained experience in a wide variety of shows and plays: Shakespeare, musical comedy, even a rock version of Hamlet! He too was introduced to Renee Valente – we have a lot to thank that lady for – and she gave him a video tape test.

For the next four years he worked in films and on Broadway, until finally the big break came. He was offered the part of David Starsky. He already knew David Soul, and the two men became great friends while working on the series. Funnily enough, although it's Hutch who scorns 'junk food' and keeps himself fit, in real life it's Paul who is the health food fan, and he enjoys yoga and meditation too. As for David, he'll eat anything good – including those sinful hamburgers and Danish pastries!

Paul Michael Glaser, who plays Starsky. No wonder he's smiling!

JUST CHAMPION!

James Hunt's blue eyes, blonde hair and dashing manner make him the perfect identikit hero, but it was his nerveless driving and grim refusal to quit when all seemed lost that won him the 1976 World Championship in the most dramatic season of motor racing the world has ever seen.

James is now reaping the financial rewards of his tremendous effort in cutting back Niki Lauda's seemingly unassailable lead. Yet his driving is as good as ever, with his split-second weighing up of percentages and cool calculation of the risks involved leaving the old image of Hunt the Shunt far behind. The reckless talent that demanded attention and began to mature under Lord Hesketh's guidance has come to fruition with the Marlboro McLaren team.

James is an all-round athlete, remembered at his school for his effortless winning of the cross country races. He has played tennis at Wimbledon as a junior and is almost international class at squash. While he admits that his knowledge of racing cars' engines is limited, his skill as a driver is unquestioned. James himself puts it down to a combination of factors rather than any mystic 'gift'.

"I've got good eyesight, though nothing really exceptional, my reflexes are pretty fair and I've got the strength to hold the car steady."

Unnecessarily modest? What do you expect from an ordinary, everyday English superstar? When James appeared with Niki Lauda at Brands Hatch after he'd won the title they were both given a standing ovation and James was mobbed wherever he went. His perseverance and bravery had earned him that adulation.

Its all go . . . Hunt arrives by helicopter at Heathrow Airport.

Hunt in a familiar pose – as victor.

Hunt's rival in their epic duel . . . Niki Lauda.

File on...

Robert Palmer

NAME: Robert Palmer

OCCUPATION: Soul singer, guitarist and songwriter

INFLUENCES: Otis Redding, who he discovered when he was fifteen; Marvin Gaye, James Brown and other soul stars.

HISTORY: Born in Batley, Yorkshire, but lived for quite a few years in Malta, where he was taught to swim by Johnny Weissmuller of *Tarzan* fame!

BANDS: First band was the Mandrakes, formed with fellow art students. While playing with them, Robert was spotted by Alan Bown, and sang with his band for a while, before joining jazz-rock band Dada. Dada was pared down to become Vinegar Joe, who enjoyed some success. Palmer left the band early in 1974 and went solo.

ALBUMS: Robert's first solo album, *Sneakin' Sally Through the Alley* was greeted as a masterpiece by critics, to be followed by *Pressure Drop* and *Some People Can Do What They Like*, which established him as a star with fans, too.

OUTLOOK: Very bright – Robert Palmer's a star!

SWIMMING SUPERSTAR

Britain's most successful sportsman at the 1976 Montreal Olympic Games was David Wilkie, lean, handsome, and a superstar swimmer.

David, from Aberdeen in Scotland, won a silver medal for Britain in the 1972 Olympics, but his sights were set on gold for 1976 – not just one medal, but two!

He spent three years at Florida's Miami University, studying English Literature and also fitting in a rigorous training schedule – over 10,000 yards a day, five days a week.

In the summer of 1976 all that work and graft paid off. In the 100 metres breaststroke final one gold medal eluded David when he was beaten into second place by his great rival John Hencken, but it was in the 200 metres breaststroke final that he really came into his own. In familiar white cap and goggles, David turned the tables on Hencken and steamed home to win the gold medal in a new world record time. No wonder he looks pleased with himself!

David Wilkie with his gold and silver Olympic medals.

Richard and

With album and single sales totalling more than thirty million, seventeen gold records – at the last count! – and concerts played to thousands of fans all over the world, the Carpenters really have worked hard on their music to earn the accolade of being called Superstars.

Richard and Karen have been a musical partnership for nearly ten years now, and in that time have recorded some of the greatest hits in recent years: *Close To You, Top of the World, Jambalaya, Goodbye to Love, Yesterday Once More* and *There's a Kind of Hush,* to name but a few. They have a devoted and ever-growing number of fans around the world, and look set for an even more successful next ten years.

Their story started in New Haven, Connecticut, where Richard, at the age of twelve, started to study the piano. He made such good progress that he went on to study the instrument at Yale, transferring to California State University when the family moved to the west coast.

Karen was also a student at the university, and when she started to play drums, she and Richard, with another student, formed the first Carpenters group, playing jazz instrumentals.

Richard became increasingly interested in composing and arranging, and the jazz group was soon disbanded in favour of a six-piece vocal group which performed original songs in very elaborate choral arrangements. But the group – called Spectrum – found little response from audiences and booking agents, and the group disbanded, leaving just Richard and Karen.

They were both becoming keen on lush, multi-voice harmonies, and worked hard on over-dubbing techniques (using their own voices) to create the depth of sound they wanted.

Their attempts were recorded in the garage studio of a friend, and the tapes sent off to Herb Alpert, of Tijuana Brass fame, the founder of A and M Records.

Herb liked what he heard, offered them a recording contract, then gave Richard and Karen the freedom to go on working on and developing their very individual style and sound.

So the pattern was set: Karen's clear, stylish vocals, backed by Richard, were captured in the studio – and hits emerged.

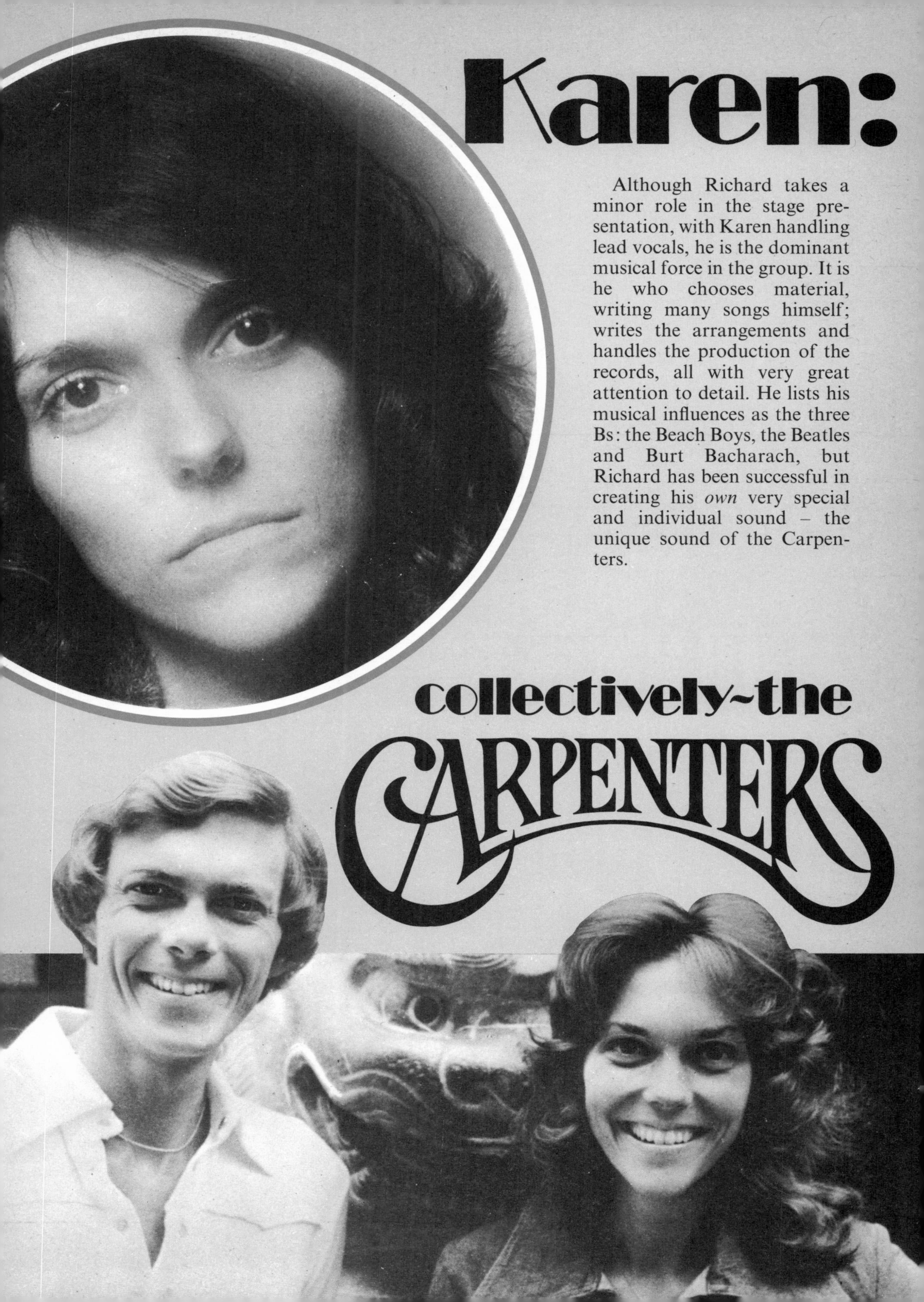

Karen:

Although Richard takes a minor role in the stage presentation, with Karen handling lead vocals, he is the dominant musical force in the group. It is he who chooses material, writing many songs himself; writes the arrangements and handles the production of the records, all with very great attention to detail. He lists his musical influences as the three Bs: the Beach Boys, the Beatles and Burt Bacharach, but Richard has been successful in creating his *own* very special and individual sound – the unique sound of the Carpenters.

collectively~the CARPENTERS

BRITAIN'S TOP TRACK GIRLS

Sonia Lannaman is Britain's best woman sprinter, and was the brightest hope for a gold medal in the 1976 Olympic Games. Her training up to the Games had gone particularly well, with Sonia recording some of the best times in the world at 100 and 200 metres, and it was thought that she had a good chance of gold medals in both her events. But tragedy struck in Canada: Sonia pulled a hamstring in training, and was out of all her events, even the 4 ×100 metres relay. But Sonia is now back, training hard, and hopes are high for her future in international athletics.

Sharon Colyear (right) of Stretford Athletics Club, is one of the brightest young hopes in British track events. She too is a sprinter, but her speciality is the 100 metres hurdles event. In Montreal there was jostling in the heat; it was re-run, and Sharon did very well to reach the semi-final. She also ran in the 4 ×100 metres relay team in the final. It was a marvellous experience for Sharon, who can only improve on her already-impressive performances.

Donna Murray is considered the pin-up girl of women's athletics, long blonde hair streaming behind her as she streaks along the track. But she's also a top-class runner, and before Montreal was ranked eighth in the world in her event, the 400 metres, behind no less than seven East German girls. She is also last-leg runner in the fast-improving British women's 4 ×100 metres relay team, and Donna is determined to go right to the top, not only in British Athletics competitions but in International circles too.

Who put the rock in Afro-rock? Osibisa, that's who! The lively African band that hit the charts in 1976 with *Sunshine Day,* closely followed by another hit, *Dance the Body Music.*

But they're not a new band. Osibisa made their first album back in 1971, and it made the top ten in the album charts. It looked as if they were destined for great things, but unfortunately there were problems within the group, and their next few releases were disappointing.

Over the years they re-organised the band, taking on several new members, and by 1975 they were ready for their new beginning. On tour, their lively act included a troop of African dancers, and the audiences loved them. This time, it looks as if Osibisa are here to stay!

Members of the band are:

TEDDY OSEI, a founder member of the band, and a big name in his native Ghana and West Africa before he came to Europe. Plays the flute, saxophone and percussion.

MAC TONTOH, younger brother of Teddy, and also an original member. Plays the trumpet, xylophone, and the flugelhorn!

SOL AMARFIO, also from Ghana. A self-taught drummer who plays bongos, maraccas and congas.

DEL RICHARDSON, lead guitarist. He left the band for a time to pursue a solo career, but now he's back with them again.

KIKI GYAN, another native of Ghana, and the band's keyboard player. He plays Moog synthesizer too, and joined in 1973.

KOFI AYIVOR, percussion and vocals. His previous experience includes work with Princess Amina, a belly dancer!

MIKE ODOMUSU, from Nigeria. He plays bass guitar, and joined the band in mid-1975 to complete the line-up.

Last year John Conteh shrugged off fifteen months of inactivity and a host of legal and financial worries to hammer Alvaro Lopez to defeat over 15 rounds in Copenhagen. John's right hand, which he damaged in Uganda, was strong enough, but he had been training so long with just his left that he found it hard to bring the right into action. The left had improved enough for John to retain his title, but there was very nearly another, unscheduled fight, before the main event.

That was when Victor Galindez, John's arch rival, sauntered into the ring and instead

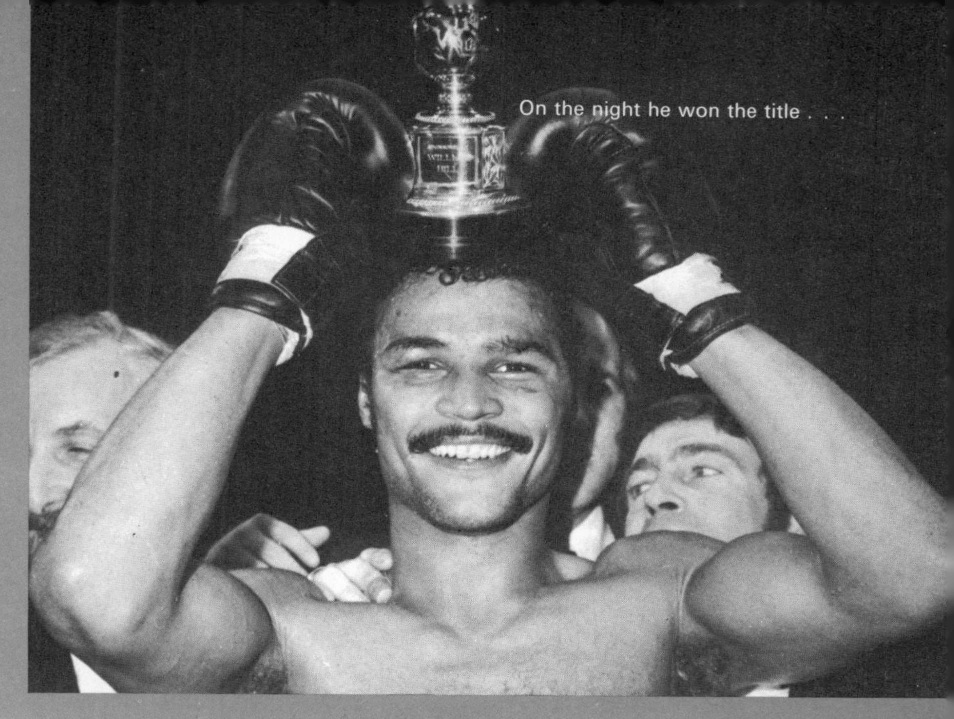

On the night he won the title . . .

GENTLEMAN JOHN!

of wishing him good luck, called him 'chicken'. George Francis saw John was about to let one go and removed Galindez as quickly as possible. Said George: "I saw John's hand twitch, and got Galindez out. If I'd had the water bottle in my hand I'd have poured it all over him."

Said John: "It was an ignorant remark to make. When Muhammad Ali does that sort of thing he does it with a smile. But not Galindez. It was the height of vulgarity. I would not dream of stooping to that level – until I fight him."

Said Galindez, when asked what he thought of John's performance: "Nothing."

When the two men meet there will be plenty of fireworks. Let's hope John can put out the Argentinian's fire and retain the World Light-Heavyweight crown. King Conteh – long may he reign!

In training . . .

PETER FRAMPTON

After lacing two Herd and five Humble Pie albums with his own very special brand of electric and acoustic guitar playing, singing and songwriting, it became clear to fans and critics alike that Peter Frampton was a force to be reckoned with. A very talented force at that . . . .

When Peter split from Humble Pie he was at first undecided as to what to do next. Finally he decided that, rather than joining someone else's band again – and there were plenty who wanted him – he would gather together a collection of good musicians and start to record solo.

This he did, and the result was as strong a debut solo album as anyone could hope to produce: *Wind of Change.*

But Peter wasn't content to carry on just working in the studios. He is an inspired live performer and, in his own words, he lives for the stage. Peter finds that the real appeal in playing his own music is being able to perform it in front of a live, receptive audience. He feels that it's the response from the fans in the concert halls and stadia that keeps his music living and breathing.

With this in mind, Peter soon took to the road with his group, Frampton's Camel, playing dates all over the country, and steadily building up a keen fan following. The hard work paid

COMES ALIVE!

Peter Frampton's band — Bob Mayo, Stanley Sheldon, John Siomos – and the man himself.

off on Peter's second solo album, called *Frampton's Camel,* which has a good, on-stage feel, even though it was recorded in the studios

More tours followed, and Peter became more and more popular in Britain and America, playing to packed houses and increasingly-enthusiastic audiences.

Which brings us to *Frampton Comes Alive* – a double album compiled from various live gigs and concerts, and presenting the very best of Peter's music, both electric and acoustic. The album topped the US charts for many, many weeks and is in fact the biggest-selling double album ever produced. It received rave reviews, and really took Peter and the band to the top of the league, followed as it was by triumphant sellout tours of America, Britain and Europe.

And the future? Peter has a wealth of writing talent, loves peforming live, and looks set to consolidate his hard-earned reputation as one of the world's most exciting rock stars. He also looks set to break into films, and has agreed to play the part of Billy Shears in the film version of *Sergeant Pepper's Lonely Hearts Club Band.* Who knows? By the time you read this, Peter Frampton may be a movie star, too!

Frampton – live!

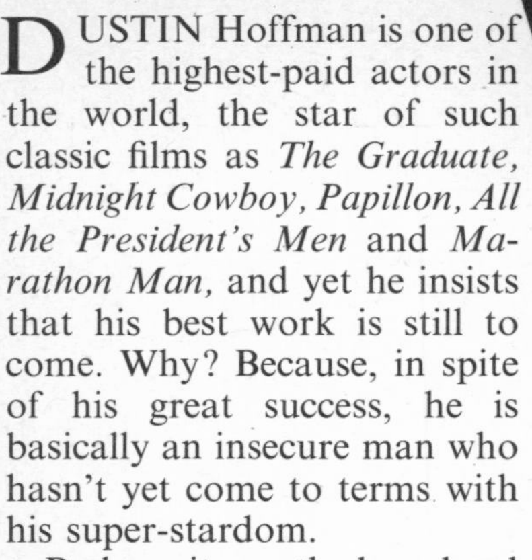

DUSTIN Hoffman is one of the highest-paid actors in the world, the star of such classic films as *The Graduate, Midnight Cowboy, Papillon, All the President's Men* and *Marathon Man,* and yet he insists that his best work is still to come. Why? Because, in spite of his great success, he is basically an insecure man who hasn't yet come to terms with his super-stardom.

Perhaps it was the long hard drag to the top that has made him so wary. He arrived, penniless, in New York, and spent eight years trying to get a job as an actor. Instead he found himself working as a mental hospital attendant, a caretaker, a pianist in a danee club, until he finally managed to get one or two bit parts in TV shows. He began to work with a community theatre too, and even taught acting for a while.

DUSTIN HOFFMAN- A RELUCTANT STAR

Finally, in 1969, he was offered a leading role in a Broadway play, but soon after rehearsals started he was badly burned in an accident, and spent six months in hospital, fighting for his life. Although he lost the part, Dustin was offered another role, in a comedy called *Eh?,* and this time there were no mishaps. One man in particular was very interested in Dustin's performance, and that was Mike Nichols, who was looking for someone to play the part of a gauche college boy in his new film. The film was *The Graduate,* and it made Dustin Hoffman a star overnight.

Suddenly everybody wanted to know him, and the offers came in thick and fast. Peace of mind was still elusive, however, and Dustin has his wife, Ann, to thank for helping him to come to terms with success. He puts his family before anything else in his life, and he reckons that without his wife and two girls, stardom would have meant nothing to him.

Now the worries and insecurities are few and Dustin is happy. He looks forward to the parts he has yet to play, and he is convinced that the work he has done so far is just the beginning. If that is so, we certainly have a lot to look forward to!

How Jack Nicholson made it in movies!

There was never any real doubt as to what Jack Nicholson wanted to do as a career: he wanted to write for, and act in, the movies. Hardly surprising when you realise that he is the son of American International Pictures chief James H. Nicholson, and grew up in an atmosphere of actors, filming and film studios.

He made a not-too-auspicious start to his career in a series of forgettable films, but really came to prominence in the very successful *Easy Rider.* Playing the part of drunken lawyer George Hanson, he earned himself a reputation as a fine actor almost overnight.

Good offers followed, and Jack went on to star in box-office hits such as *Five Easy Pieces, The Last Detail, The Missouri Breaks, Chinatown* and *One Flew Over the Cuckoo's Nest.* He has also tried his hand at writing and directing, but these films have not been very successful. Be that as it may, Jack Nicholson has firmly established himself as one of *the* film faces of the 1970s.

RIGHT ON CUE

Radcliffe's own John Spencer. A firm bridge, cue lined up and his eye on the ball.

Prowess at snooker used to be regarded as a sign of misspent youth, the argument being that excellence could only be achieved by long hours of truancy spent in dimly-lit snooker halls. Nowadays snooker has lost its wide-boy image and is one of the fastest growing sports in Britain.

Why the turnaround in snooker's previously declining fortunes? American pool tables, with their emphasis on potting skill and cue-ball control have helped. So has the hooliganism, pathetic crowd facilities and lack lustre football found at many soccer grounds. But the main reason for the snowballing interest in what was once the strictly 'men only' preserve of huge dark halls and working men's clubs, is the excellent promotion of today's game and the willingness of older snooker fans to teach youngsters the game. There are two snooker programmes on television, challenge matches, new leagues and knock-out tournaments, pro-celebrity competitions and an increased coverage in the press.

Snooker's boom has pushed its stars into national prominence. John Spencer, Eddie Charlton, Ray Reardon and Alex Higgins are the best known. Alex 'the Hurricane' startled the staid snooker world when he lifted the World Championship in his early twenties, earning his nickname from his non-stop style of play.

Eddie Charlton is more professional in his approach. Whereas Alex will pot away whatever the conditions, Charlton will protest if he feels they put him at a disadvantage. He is a shrewd player and currently the world's most successful. He is an excellent ambassador for the game.

So is John Spencer. He rose from anonymity in the Radcliffe leagues to take the 1971 world crown, and before the arrival of Alex Higgins was one of the youngest champions for some time. John is a gentleman with a sharp sense of humour and a relaxed approach that helps him keep his confidence. There seems little doubt that he will win back the world crown some time in the future, but everyone playing today would be lucky if they did just half as well as 'The Greatest', snooker's very first superstar Joe Davis. Joe was undefeated champion from 1926 until his retirement in 1946. Beat that, lads!

Eddie Charlton checks out the angle on the cushion.

BIG BREN – Gateshead's Iron Man

Every week, on 'club night' at the Gateshead Harriers Club, a collection of people, ranging from young schoolboys to pensioners, turn up to train. Some take a steady jog around the track, others run up the punishing grassy hills that surround it, while the hard men take to the roads, thinking nothing of clocking up fifteen miles in a night's running.

One of the hard men, and the Harriers Club star, is Brendan Foster.

Brendan probably started his career in athletics when he used to run home from school in time to watch the 1960 Olympic Games on television. Later he ran in English schools championships, and cross-country races while at university. But it wasn't until the summer of 1973, when he moved up to the 5,000 metre distance from the mile and won the European Cup Final, that his running gained true International significance.

Brendan soon became the great crowd-puller (along with David Bedford, of course) in British athletics. He likes to run out front, setting the pace, and it's his amazing ability to make punishing and repeated mid-race sprints that impresses, and worries, many of his rivals.

He likes to 'break' the pack with those sprints of his, and carefully drawn-up plans are made with his coach, Stan Long, days and weeks before important races. He likes to 'feel' the pace of a race, try to estimate how much running his rivals have left in them, then make his move.

Brendan made it to Montreal as a gold-medal hope in both his events: the 5,000 and 10,000 metres, but his Canadian training was interrupted by an unpleasant stomach bug. Nevertheless, he made it to the final of the 10,000 metres.

The race was run as never before: Brendan made no dramatic mid-race breaks, but managed to cling onto the third place behind Viren and Lopes. He was clearly weakened by the stomach trouble, but nevertheless won what was to be Britain's only track medal.

Brendan's prospects in the shorter race looked good: he had set a new Olympic record of 13 minutes 20.34 seconds in one of the heats, and was thought to be recovering from his illness. But he never found the strength or power that he needed, and finished fifth in the race.

Nevertheless, Brendan's achievement was one to be proud of, and he returned home to a hero's welcome. He is very definitely Gateshead's favourite son and, as they say with some pride in the North-east, 'a right good rooner'.

Rumanian Rhapsody

Can you improve on perfection? That must be what the world's gymnasts were saying after Nadia Comaneci's wonderful display in the 1976 Olympics. This slim, supple Rumanian girl achieved Olympic history when she scored ten points for her routine on the asymmetric bars. Perfection indeed!

Ever since 1972, when Olga Korbut sparked off a world-wide interest in gymnastics, the sport has become more and more popular. Thus, when the Olympics began, millions of viewers waited expectantly for some spectacular entertainment, and they weren't disappointed. They had already seen something of Nadia Comaneci in previous competitions – she won the European championship in 1975 – but she was to surpass all expectations with her faultless routines.

The Russian girls put up a good fight, and they succeeded in winning the team gold, while Rumania came second. But when it came to the individual events they must have known in their hearts that the 14 year old Nadia was a serious threat to their supremacy. While they got good marks – Olga Korbut scored 9.80 on the beam – Nadia did better. While the Russians charmed the judges with their smiles and waves, Nadia Comaneci performed with such technical brilliance that they could find no fault. She scored her second ten on the asymmetric bars, and her third on the beam.

Nadia Comaneci was discovered at the age of seven, playing in a school playground with her friends. Her agility and courage were so obvious that she was chosen to train for the Rumanian team. For one so young she has remarkable self-control, as can be seen in

A pose full of impish charm as Nadia Comaneci performs her floor exercise.

She flies through the air with the greatest of ease . . . Nadia finishes her exercise on the beam with a flourish.

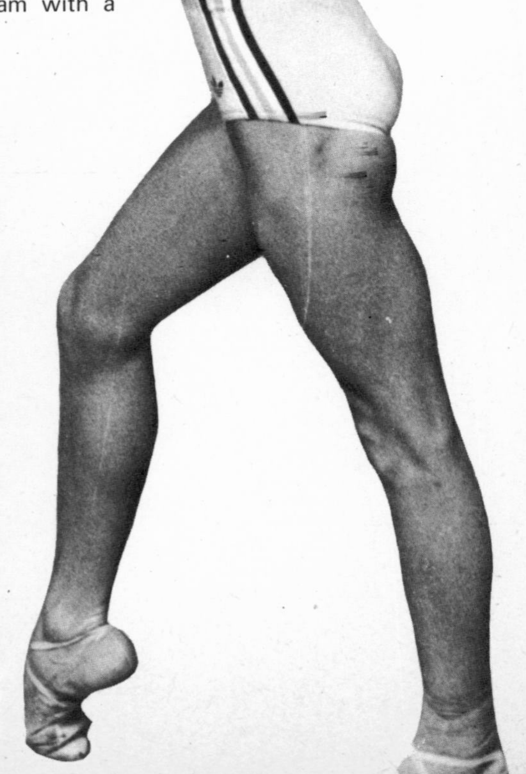

Part of the faultless routine that brought Nadia Comaneci the first of her perfect scores.

Grace and balance in a beautifully controlled handstand.

the way she performed her very first Olympic exercise. It was on the beam, the most technically demanding of the apparatus, and she could have been forgiven for showing slight nervousness and hesitation. But there was none. She began as she meant to go on, scoring 9.90, and winning the respect and applause of the Russian girls as well as the audience.

It has been said that her routines are too stark, too lacking in emotion, but it must be remembered that she is still very young, and experience will probably mellow that slightly clinical brilliance into something warmer, but no less bright.

Rhymin' Simon

It isn't often that a member of a highly successful pop group can achieve the same success as a solo artist, but Paul Simon has shown that it can be done. As the songwriting member of the duo, Simon and Garfunkel, he was one of the most popular artistes of the sixties, and when the duo split he continued to make successful records, if anything improving on his original work with Art Garfunkel.

He teamed up with Art Garfunkel in 1964 and they began the partnership that was to last through the sixties. They sang folk and protest songs, and at first they weren't very good. Paul made a solo trip to Britain, and here he enjoyed minor success in the folk clubs, and recorded *The Paul Simon Songbook*. However, back in the U.S.A. *The Sound Of Silence* had been released as a single, and by the time he returned the record was a number one hit.

Since then there has been no looking back, and Paul Simon's work improves with every album. From his early folk songs he has broadened his style to embrace a variety of musical styles, although his words have the same poetic, searching and personal quality.

Solo albums *Paul Simon* and *There Goes Rhymin' Simon* contain some of his best work, and it looks as if Rhymin' Simon can only improve.

Let's go latin!

EVERY music lover knows that a Latin rhythm is irresistible, but combined with rock it's Santana, the band who have led the field in Latin-rock for ten years or more.

The founder of the band, Carlos Santana, was born in Mexico, and he grew up with the Latin American beat in his blood. After working in various tequila mills and night-clubs he moved to San Francisco, and here he formed an electric blues band. However, there were many similar bands trying to make the grade and to make his own more distinctive, Carlos introduced several Latin musicians into the band, and so produced his commercial brand of Latin-rock.

Success was almost immediate, and although the Santana line-up has changed over the years, the standard of music has remained the same. Carlos Santana's own brilliance on guitar is renowned in the musical world, and the pure, tonal quality he achieves has contributed much to the band's success. Whether soft and soulful, like *Samba Pa Ti,* or earthy like *Black Magic Woman,* the Latin influence is there, and the band makes full use of percussion to produce the infectious foot-tapping sound.

Their concerts are a sell-out wherever they go, and in late 1976 they recorded a special concert for the B.B.C. They have bridged the gap between the sixties and the seventies and, who knows, they may carry on into the eighties too!

ASK anyone who *the* greatest male athlete at the 1976 Montreal Olympics was, and you can be almost sure they'll name Finland's Lasse Viren. For the second time in four years he took on the very best of the world's long-distance runners – and beat them convincingly, thus becoming the first man in history to retain his two Olympic titles. Even the successes of Juantorena of Cuba and America's Ed Moses must be over-shadowed by Viren's magnificent performance.

Brendan Foster storms home in heat three of the 5,000 metres in a new Olympic record time.

THE LONG-

Lasse Viren salutes the crowd after his great win in the 10,000 metres.

Story of a Long-Distance Runner

Lasse Viren followed in a long tradition of quality Finnish long-distance running. He grew up hearing the names of national heroes like Paavo Nurmi and Hannes Holehmainen – the Flying Finns – and determined to make his name not just as *a* Flying Finn, but as *the* Flying Finn.

This he did in spectacular style at the Munich Olympic Games in 1972. He succeeded in winning both 5,000 and 10,000 metre gold medals, despite a crashing fall in the final of the 10,000 metre race. He collided with the Tunisian runner Gammoudi, but recovered, and stormed home in first place. It says something for the calibre and style of the runner that he was able to make up precious seconds lost in the fall and still win easily – in a new world record time.

Viren was back again at the 1976 Games in Montreal. His build-up to the Games had been quiet, with little publicity, and in fact his successes in International competitions had been few and far between in the years after Munich.

The first of the long-distance

races was the 10,000 metres. The race was run in unexpected style: there were no fast breaks by Britain's great hope Brendan Foster, and the pace was set by a relatively unknown Portugese runner Carlos Lopes. Lopes led the field for a great part of the race, knowing that he had no finishing sprint speed, and hoping to wear down the opposition with punishing lap speeds. But Viren was always with him, breathing down his neck, and just over a lap from the finish the Finn sprinted into a lead that he kept up to the winning tape.

Viren had successfully defended one of his Munich titles, and the other athletes running in the final were determined that he shouldn't win the other final in which he was entered, the 5,000 metres.

Viren makes his way through the field to complete his two gold-medal wins in the 1976 Olympics.

DISTANCE MEN

At an early stage of the 5,000 metres final, Britain's Brendan Foster and Ian Stewart lead the field.

Trouble was, no one knew how to beat him. It was his hardest race of the four, but he once again stormed home to cross the winning tape ahead of New Zealand's Dick Quax and West Germany's Klaus-Peter Hildebrand.

Even that success wasn't enough for the Finn. He entered the punishing Marathon, and did extremely well to finish fifth, a great performance after his two hard finals just days before.

Lasse Viren succeeded in becoming *the* Flying Finn, and one of the greatest distance runners of all time, and who knows? – he may be back to defend his titles in 1980!

IAN ANDERSON- the singer with the band

Ian Anderson *is* Jethro Tull. He formed the band back in 1968, and he has been the leading figure ever since.

Anderson is a showman, a colourful character who prances across the stage in a series of postures and poses, but he is also an excellent musician, playing the flute, the guitar and keyboard instruments. He is also the vocalist with Jethro Tull, and to cap it all he composes most of their material himself: strong, melodic songs with plenty of racy wit, comments on life as he sees it.

Anderson's personality is evident in his stage costumes – vivid silks and satins that make him look more like the Pied Piper than a progressive rock star!

After the initial success of the band in this country they went to America, and for a time they were criticised for deserting their British fans. However, Jethro Tull returned with a highly successful tour in late 1974/75, and all was forgiven. Now they concentrate mainly on album material, although they have had several hit singles in the past, including *Living in the Past, Witche's Promise* and *Life is a Long Song.*

Super STEELEYE!

A collection of individuals, that's Steeleye Span. Capable of perfect harmony together, and yet each one talented in his, or her, own right. Over the years, Steeleye have established an enviable reputation in the music world with their distinctive brand of folk-rock, and now they are proving they can work just as well apart.

But before you start to worry that the band is splitting up, you will be pleased to know that they still regard Steeleye as their main outlet, with individual interests and projects running alongside. Maddy Prior, whose hauntingly-sweet voice has become the focal point of the band, recently teamed up with June Tabor to record *Silly Sisters,* an album which returned to the gentler, more folksey sound of early Steeleye.

Peter Knight and Bob Johnson, fiddler and guitarist respectively, have been working on a highly imaginative project. They have made a 'fantasy album' based on a book called *The King of Elfland's Daughter,* with narration by that master of fantasy, Christopher Lee.

Flautist and drummer Nigel Pegrum has formed his own record label to cater for folk club acts, and Rick Kemp and Tim Hart are involved in record production.

Olympic Track Stars

Two of the outstanding male athletics stars of the 1976 Montreal Olympics were New Zealand's John Walker and Jamaica's Don Quarrie. Here's how they won those coveted gold medals:

Don Quarrie: 200 metres

Don Quarrie was favourite to win this event in Munich, but didn't even finish among the medals. 1976 was his second chance at the gold, and this time he made no mistake. Quarrie was already world record holder and Commonwealth champion, and with the elimination of Steve Williams, Quarrie's only real rival for the gold was Trinidad's Haseley Crawford. Crawford had beaten Quarrie into second place in the final of the 100 metres, and he was out looking for his second gold medal when the final started.

Crawford soon pulled up after a bad start, and that left the race open for Quarrie to storm to the tape ahead of Americans Millard Hampton and Dwayne Evans. Munich's failure had become Montreal's success.

Don Quarrie (574) finishes ahead of Americans Hampton and Evans.

John Walker: 1,500 metres

The 1,500 metres is perhaps the Olympic competition that attracts more attention than any other, and Montreal was no exception. It was thought by many that Bayi's withdrawal would leave the way clear for New Zealand's John Walker, but when Walker was eliminated from the heats of the 800 metres through illness, observers felt that the final was wide open.

The heats didn't give much away as to the quality of the finalists, but Ireland's Eamonn Coghlan put in good times, and was favoured to test Walker in the final. This proved true, with Coghlan leading for much of the race. But just before the start of the last lap Walker overhauled the Irish runner and accelerated steadily away from the rest of the field. He ran a stylish, comfortable race that really showed his world class, and crossed the line in a time of 3 mins 39.17 seconds ahead of Vandamme of Belgium and Wellmann of Germany.

Jubilation from John Walker as he crosses the line to win the gold medal in the 1,500 metres.

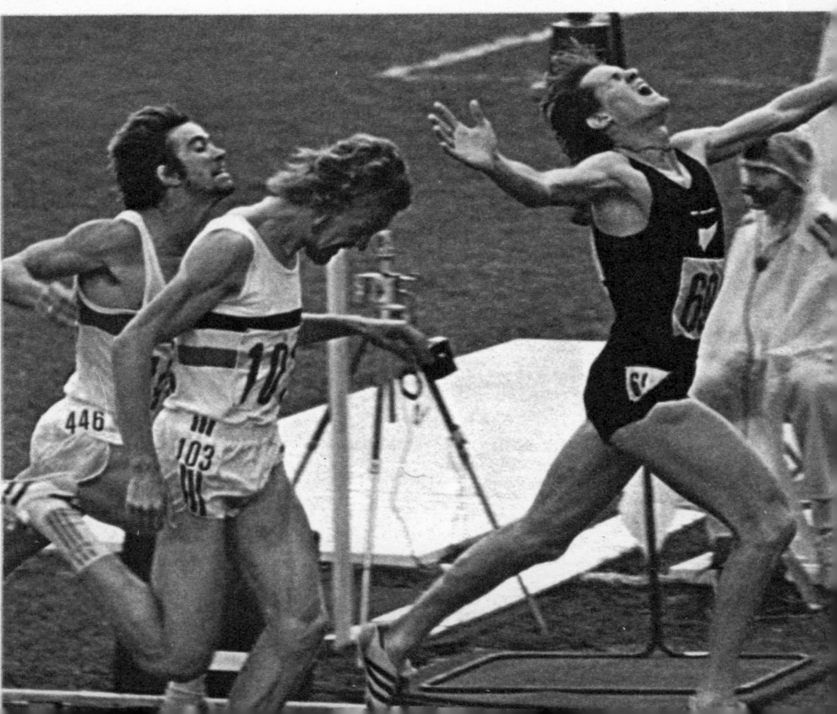

File on...
Robin Trower

NAME: Robin Trower

OCCUPATION: One of world's leading rock guitarists

HISTORY: Was member of Procol Harum, then left to form own band, Jude, with ex Jethro Tull member Clive Bunker and Jim Dewar, formerly of Stone the Crows. Jude was disbanded, and Robin Trower Band came into being.

INFLUENCES: Blues, and Jimi Hendrix, to whom many critics have compared his style.

ALBUMS: Many and varied, from the early *Twice Removed from Yesterday* down to *Long Misty Days,* mostly made up of self-penned material.

OUTLOOK: Looks good. Robin is still more popular in the US than in his native Britain, but album sales here are increasing, and tours are sell-outs. Looks like building on his hard-earned reputation as one of the world's best rock guitarists.

SOCCER'S STROLLING PLAYERS

Troublesome troubadors – or soccer's last hope? When George Best got sent off within a month of his come-back season the knives came out ready sharpened. When Fulham's opening season burst began to fade, the hecklers turned on Rodney Marsh for his lack of effort, and armchair pundits were quick to remember how the League Championship was within Manchester City's grasp when Marsh arrived, and eight games later they had lost it. Stories of his riding onto the field on the back of an elephant with Tampa Bay Rowdies did little to reassure those who thought Marsh had more flash than class. The two players were undoubtedly skilful, but should there be a place for them in today's game?

Of course there should. Best is a football genius so rare that it would be criminal to deny thousands of fans with money to spend the chance of going to see him. Fulham have breathed some welcome fresh air into the Second Division, and the crowds they draw, both home and away, are proof that they are giving the fans what they want. Best has shown at International level that he can still live with the best, and it

George Best attacks the Wolves defence with Rodney Marsh in close support.

Marsh swings one in.

Best . . . on his way back to peak fitness.

Marsh slips a defender en route for goal.

would be a shame if his past record were used to lever him out of the game. He is in demand to play all over the world, but he came back to Britain to play for a Second Division team. As he himself says: "This is the first club I've played for where they've treated me like an adult."

Alec Stock is no fool. He stressed to the players before he signed them that the good name of Fulham was the first of his priorities. Best has responded with some marvellous moments of football magic.

Marsh has had his moments too. Rodney would be the first to admit that his thinking is not in step with the rest of the football world. Anyone who's seen him in a natty three-piece suit, sharp shirt and no socks might imagine his off-the-field thinking is something less than conventional.

They'd be right. Marsh is an eccentric. Intelligent, eloquent, good-natured, the football field is a stage to Marsh, not a battlefield. It is an attitude that has irritated many fans and players alike, but his belief that football should be more fun is a genuine one, and it takes courage to stick with such a belief when people on all sides reject it. As one disconsolate Manchester City fan said after Marsh's departure to America: "We'll win more matches, sure – but do you think that's all I come here for?"

Maybe Fulham won't win any of soccer's major trophies, but they are winning plenty of friends on the terraces with their cavalier approach. Signing Marsh and Best was not only a shrewd move financially, it gave thousands of young fans the chance to see two of football's most highly gifted players, each with his own view on how the game should be played. And in a game as regulated as football that can't be bad.

BIG NAMES OF THE SHOWRING

Harvey Smith on Speakeasy, sailing over a Hickstead fence.

Harvey on Olympic Star at the Horse of the Year Show.

To say that Harvey Smith is a bit of a character is a great understatement. He's a showman, wrestler, chat-show guest of note, farmer, trainer and, on top of all that, one of the world's top show jumping stars.

Smith is a straight-talking Yorkshireman from Bingley who might clown around outside the ring, but who takes his show jumping career very seriously indeed.

That career started in 1954. Harvey was already an experienced rider when he bought a horse called Farmer's Boy for £40, and determined to make a jumper out of him. This he did, and the partnership was such a success that horse and rider were chosen to ride with the British team in Dublin in 1958.

Harvey has always trained his own horses, and is acknowledged as a very fine trainer: hard and firm, but always ready to reward effort in his mounts. His horses are a catalogue of fine jumpers: O'Malley, Volvo, Speakeasy, Olympic Star, Madison Time and many, many more.

The West Germans have been producing top show jumpers for many years, and one of their most consistent and popular riders is Alwin Schockemohle. Like all top German show jumping stars, he rides big, strong Hanoverian horses which have the perfect build and temperament to be schooled for jumping and dressage work.

Alwin is first and foremost a farmer, and classes show jumping as his hobby, but he is

Alwin Schockemohle and Warwick Rex on their way to a gold medal in the Montreal Olympics.

so successful that competitions and meetings take up most of his time, especially in the summer.

He first jumped abroad in 1960, and since then has been a very frequent and popular visitor to British shows and contests, winning almost all the major International titles on fine horses such as The Robber and Warwick Rex.

In fact it was on Warwick that Alwin had perhaps his best win of all – an individual gold medal in the show jumping competition in the 1976 Olympic Games.

Alwin and Donald Rex negotiate the famous Derby Bank at Hickstead.

David Broome's great achievements in the world of show jumping are legendary. His great riding talent and his ability in choosing and bringing on talented horses has been rewarded with wins in every important show jumping competition at home and abroad.

His career spans more than two decades, in which he has won the World Championship title, the European Championship title, plus many other trophies and honours. The only award missing from his collection is perhaps a gold Olympic medal. He won bronze in 1968 on Mr Softee, but was excluded from competing in the 1976 Games as he is no longer considered an amateur.

David farms in Wales, where he takes a great interest in selecting and training horses. His skill in bringing on inexperienced horses has led to marvellous partnerships between David and his horses; remember Mr Softee, Ballywillwill, Beethoven and Heatwave?

Throughout David's long career in show jumping he has maintained his own high standards, and looks set to stay at the top for many more years.

David Broome and Heatwave competing in the Embassy International Grand Prix.

Stan's the man!

You can imagine Stan Bowles' delight when George Poyser, manager of the Manchester City team he had been supporting since the age of thirteen, offered to sign him on. Stan put his name on the dotted line and began a career that was to plumb some miserable depths before rising on a wave of controversy to the dizzying heights of international stardom.

To look at, Stan Bowles doesn't seem capable of rousing the indignance, anger and even outrage he has done among football's more self righteous writers and fans. He is clear eyed, confident, eminently likeable, and laughs with the ease of a man who knows where he is going.

The picture in his early days with City was not so clear. Poyser left, Joe Mercer arrived and Malcolm Allison came soon after. City won promotion from the Second Division and started on five years of almost unbroken success. With a forward line of Summerbee, Bell, Lee, Young and Coleman, there wasn't much chance for Stan to shine. He began to fall out with Mercer and eventually he went to Bury on a free transfer. He lasted three weeks at Bury and then moved on another free to Crewe Alexandra.

Stan enjoyed his spell in the Fourth Division, but when Carlisle came in with a bid of £12,000 he left. In 33 games with Carlisle he scored 11 goals to finish joint top scorer for the season. His play had attracted the attention of Gordon Jago, then manager of Queen's Park Rangers, who had the money from the sale of Rodney Marsh burning a hole in his pocket. Jago was ambitious for Rangers, and when he signed Bowles for £112,000, and teamed him up with Venables, Thomas, Givens and Francis, they took the Second Division by storm.

In time Dave Sexton replaced Jago, and Rangers developed into one of the most progressive and entertaining teams in the land.

Maybe it was the sound of Malcolm Macdonald blowing his own trumpet over at Highbury, or the desire to win back his England place, or merely the natural result of several years steady improvement, but last season Bowles came into his own, startling defences both at home and abroad with his skill. He equalled a E.U.F.A. scoring record and left First Division defenders sprawling on the ground. For those who like their football rich in character it was a treat.

Stan has come a long way since those early days at City. If you were asked to make a list of the most brilliant, exciting footballers of the last five years the chances are that it wouldn't be a long one. But one name deserves a place on any such list: England's finest striker, Stan Bowles.

Bowles . . . an original.

THAT OLD WHITE MAGIC

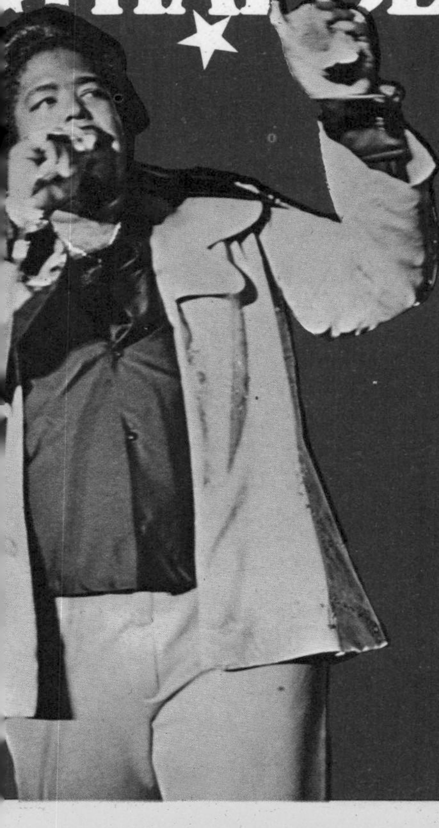

Barry White: a big man with a big sound and an even bigger following of loyal fans. Lush, romantic ballads sung in that rich, deep voice are his speciality, and the fans keep asking for more.

Singing is only the most recent outlet for White's musical talent. Until 1972 he was writing and producing records for other soul artistes, including such classics as *Harlem Shuffle* by Bob and Earl, *I Feel Love Comin' On* by Felice Taylor, and *Walkin' In The Rain With The One I Love* by Love Unlimited.

Then, with the latter as his backing group and the Love Unlimited Orchestra providing the strings, Barry recorded *I'm Gonna Love You Just A Little Bit More Baby.* The song was a big hit, and so was the follow-up, *Never Gonna Give You Up.* After this, a string of hit singles followed, each in the inimitable White style, and discos all over the country were playing them to delighted fans. His British tour was a great success too, and Barry can be sure of a great welcome on future visits.

He has been criticised for sticking to the same kind of sound for each single, but his records keep selling, and while they appear in the charts, Barry White will keep on giving the public what they want.

SUPERSTARS COMPETITION

Enter our easy competition and you could win our super first prize of a trip to a T.V. studio, all expenses paid, for you and a parent, guardian or friend. All you have to do is answer the simple questions below, and also tell us which superstar you think we should have included in our annual, and why. The answers to the questions can all be found in the annual so it couldn't be easier. Runners-up will receive a record token.

1. Who took the male lead in Ken Russell's film *The Boyfriend*?

2. What was the name of Maddy Prior's partner on the album *Silly Sisters*?

3. What was David Soul's stage name before he took up acting?

4. From which country do the majority of the members of the band Osibisa come?

5. Which club made an offer for Chelsea captain Butch Wilkins?

6. Where did David Wilkie study English Literature?

7. Name the club that Brendan Foster runs for.

8. Name Richard Meade's horse in the 1972 Olympics.

9. Lasse Viren won two gold medals at the 1976 Olympics. What were they for?

10. How old was Björn Borg when he was first picked for the Swedish Davis Cup team?

Send your answers, together with your name, age, and address to:

Superstars Competition,
World Distributors Ltd.,
P.O. Box 111,
Manchester M60 1TS.

All entries must be received by 30th March, 1978.

Eventing Superstar

Meade rides Jacob Jones on his way to yet another Olympic medal – this time a bronze in Montreal.

No other sport has mushroomed in popularity in recent years as suddenly as three-day eventing. From rough and ready meetings attended by just a few stalwart supporters, the sport has grown into an important spectator event, attracting thousands of fans.

To enthusiasts the attraction of the sport is easily understood: it is considered the finest trial of all-round horsemanship, taking in strict dressage, tough cross-country riding and a show jumping section.

Richard Meade is the undisputed champion of British three-day eventing. From riding in Pony Club competitions when he was a child in Monmouthshire, he graduated to a place in the British team at an international students' meeting, found himself on the winning team, and has never looked back.

Soon after he was again chosen to represent Britain – this time at the Tokyo Olympics in 1964. Wins in major British and European events followed, before Meade was again chosen to ride in the Olympic team – this time in Mexico.

He rode Cornishman V across a treacherous cross-country section to finish with the third highest bonus points of the day, then rode a good show jumping round to ensure that the British team won the gold medal. In fact, Richard only narrowly missed winning an individual medal too, finishing fourth overall.

Perhaps Richard's finest hour came with yet another Olympic appearance – Munich in 1972. Riding Laurieston, he was in superb form. His control in the highly-disciplined dressage section, strength in the cross-country section and perfect round in the final show jumping section earned Richard the individual gold medal. Not only that, his marvellous form earned the team enough points to secure the team gold too, making Richard the first Englishman to win two gold medals at one Games.

Even after such a fine career, Richard Meade was in no mood for retiring, and he appeared at yet another Games – Montreal in 1976! This time he rode Jacob Jones, and completed a clear cross-country round for the fourth time in a row in the Olympics, all on different horses.

With two riders retired, the British team was out of the running, but Meade still had a chance of an individual award, and this he snatched in the show jumping ring – a very creditable bronze medal to add to his collection.

After many years of top competition, Meade still holds the crown as Britain's top eventer – perhaps he'll even ride in the Moscow Olympics . . .

Richard Meade on his way to individual and team golds in the 1972 Olympic Games.

Richard Meade on one of his famous horses, Laurieston.

THE MANY FACES OF GENE WILDER

Gene Wilder, with his co-star, Madeline Kahn, in a scene from *The Adventures of Sherlock Holmes' Smarter Brother.*

Gene Wilder, he of the sideways grin and the popping, surprised eyes, was once described as a (slightly) saner version of Harpo Marx. He is undoubtedly one of the finest comic actors ever produced, but he has other talents, too: writing screenplays and directing his own films. And he does all of these things very, very successfully.

He started off acting while at university in America, then came to England and played with the Bristol Old Vic company for a time. Back in New York he found work hard to come by and took on a variety of jobs: chauffeur, fencing instructor (he had found time while in England to become a champion fencer) and shop assistant in the toy department of a large store; no doubt storing up a wealth of comic pieces to be used in his later work.

His luck started to change when he found success in a number of Broadway theatre roles, and film parts were offered to him. The first to bring him into the public eye was probably the role of Eugene Grizzard in the hugely-successful *Bonnie and Clyde.* He then co-starred in Mel Brooks' *The Producers* and played opposite Donald Sutherland in *Start the Revolution Without Me,* carrying off both comic roles with great style.

He branched out into writing screenplays, as well as directing and acting in films, and the box-office successes flowed thick and fast: the highly-amusing Western spoof, *Blazing Saddles; Young Frankenstein,* with Marty Feldman, and *The Adventures of Sherlock Holmes' Smarter Brother.* All his films are very funny – and all are very successful.

The many facets of Gene Wilder's talent go to make him that rare thing today – an all-round star of the cinema.

A very together group!

For many years now the Eurovision Song Contest has been a showcase for the talents of singers and song-writers in many countries of the world. New stars emerge each year, but few have achieved the continuing success of the 1974 winners, Abba.

Abba won the contest with the song *Waterloo,* which was a catchy, sing-along number, of the type which are always popular entries. It was a big hit, and the pop world waited in interest to see what would happen next.

Ring, Ring, Mamma Mia, and the later *Dancing Queen* were all big hits, in a similar style to *Waterloo.* But the wistful *Fernando,* which tells the story of a freedom fighter in the Spanish Civil War, proved that they can competently handle songs which are much more difficult to perform than pure 'pop' numbers.

Their name comes from the initials of all four members – Agnetha (known as Anna), Bjorn, Benny and Annifrid (known as Frida). In their personal lives as well as on stage, they're very much a group. Bjorn is married to Anna, and at the time of going to press, Benny is engaged to Frida. They all live in the same suburb of Stockholm, and they spend their holidays together too, on an island in Stockholm's archipelago, where they are all keen sailors.

As you can see, in more ways than one, they're a very together group.

REMEMBER THE OLYMPICS?

HOW MUCH DO YOU REMEMBER ABOUT THE 1976 OLYMPIC GAMES IN MONTREAL? HERE'S A CROSSWORD TO TEST YOUR MEMORY ON THE SPORTSMEN AND WOMEN WHO COMPETED THERE.

CLUES ACROSS:

1. The country where the 'Flying Finn' of 1976 comes from (7)
5. . . . . Korbut, Russian gymnastics star (4)
7. see 6 down
10. Champion swimmer Kornelia Ender comes from . . . . Germany (4)
11. . . Moses, US hurdler (2)
13. The colour of medal for competitors taking second place in a final (6)
14. Abbreviation for American team (2)
17. see 8 down
18. . . . . . Wilkie, Britain's medal-winning swimmer (5)

CLUES DOWN:

1. Jim . . ., captain of Britain's gold medal-winning pentathlon team (3)
2. . . . . . Comaneci, women's gymnastics champion at only fourteen (5)
3. Royal Olympic competitor (4)
4. Dick . . . ., New Zealand runner (4)
6. and 7 across. The 'Flying Finn' of the Montreal Olympics (5, 5)
8. and 17 across. Russian gymnastics star (5, 3)
9. . . . . athlon is a competition composed of five elements (4)
12. Abbreviations for Russia (4)
15. . . . Dixon, New Zealand star (3)
16. Russian super-heavyweight weight lifter, gold medallist in Montreal – initials only (2)

ANSWERS

Across: 1. Finland; 5. Olga; 7. Viren; 10. East; 11. Ed; 13. Silver; 14. US; 17. Kim; 18. David.
Down: 1. Fox; 2. Nadia; 3. Anne; 4. Quax; 6. Lasse; 8. Nelli; 9. Pent; 12. USSR; 15. Rod; 16. VA (Vasili Alexeev)

Rick Wakeman is a musician in the grand manner. His music, his concerts, his life-style: all are slightly larger than life, thanks to his vivid imagination and enormous talent.

There is great breadth of vision in his music, with jazz, rock and classical influences, and the combination of imagination and a sound musical training has produced such fine albums as *The Six Wives of Henry VIII, Journey to the Centre of the Earth, The Myths and Legends of King Arthur and the Knights of the Round Table,* and *No Earthly Connection.*

Rick's grand vision extends to presentation too, and early performances of these works were rock spectaculars on a huge scale. He used large orchestras, choirs and special effects, with his own English Rock Ensemble backing band. In an open air performance of *Journey* he had huge inflatable prehistoric monsters leaping out of a lake, while for *King Arthur* he staged a three-day ice pageant . . . both at great expense.

RICK WAKEMAN~ a grand master

Since then, productions have been less extravagant, although Rick still believes that his audiences should be entertained visually as well as musically. He believes in giving his all too, and to such an extent that he suffered a minor heart attack after staging *Journey to the Centre of the Earth.*

As a keyboard player Rick Wakeman is one of the best, and every year he figures in the music papers' polls for both his albums and his brilliant playing. Many people consider him to be the finest rock organist in the world, and he is certainly popular from Japan to Brazil, from America to Australia. He makes a lot of money too, and he is the head of a large business empire, including a car hire firm which runs his collection of Rolls Royces, eight at the last count.

Rick began his career as a session musician, after a disastrous year at the Royal College of Music, but after meeting Strawbs' leader Dave Cousins he joined the band, playing with them for fifteen months. But he is best remembered for his dynamic keyboard playing with the band, Yes. He stayed with them for three years, leaving in 1974 to follow a solo career. However, in December 1976, Rick surprised the music

world by rejoining Yes to work on a new album, and also to tour with them. On the solo side, his career continued with the release of *White Rock,* the soundtrack for a film about the 1976 Winter Olympics.

Rick is an ambitious man, and he works hard to achieve music he really believes and feels, and which will, at the same time, appeal to a wide audience. His popularity in the album charts shows that he has achieved this aim, and with his great talent for both writing and playing, it looks as if he will be there for some time.

She's done it again! A triumphant Chrissy holds her Wimbledon trophy aloft.

Chris

Cool, calm, and collected, that's Chris Evert, and this unflappable nature has earned her the title of 'Little Miss Cool'. It has also helped to make her the best woman tennis player in the world, together with her great determination and powerful style.

She is one of several young players who have adopted the two-handed stroke, and while it is not the most elegant style in the world, it is certainly one of the most effective. Her back hand in particular is very powerful, and has often got her out of trouble and into an attacking position. Chris likes to play from the back of the court, and her accurate lobs and beautifully placed passing shots are real winners.

Chris, or Chrissy as she is called, began playing on the international tennis circuit when she was sixteen, and within three years she had won that most coveted of all tennis titles, Wimbledon. Since then she has won both singles and doubles titles, as well as most of the other major championships round the world. Critics say that she is too machine-like on court, but if that's the way to win, why should she care? Emotions are best kept away from the game, and once she starts to play, Chrissy has only one thing on her mind, and that is winning.

If all this sounds a little too tough, Chrissy softens the image with some of the prettiest tennis dresses around, and she usually wears jewellery on court too. Not for her the rather masculine shorts that her predecessor, Billy Jean King, used to favour although, like Billy Jean, she is a great believer in women's rights in the game.

Evert

Above: Deep concentration as Chrissy plays that famous two-handed backhand.

Left: Another two-handed shot, and you can see that Chrissy really means to win!

BJÖRN BORG

The new champion. A happy Björn Borg displays his Wimbledon trophy.

The defeated Ilie Nastase embraces Björn as they leave the court.

This blonde, good-looking Swedish boy has become one of the most popular players on the tennis scene, especially with the ladies, but beneath the heart-throb image Björn is one of the best tennis players in the world. His temperament is ideal for the game, and in spite of his youth he manages to keep calm in matches against older and more experienced players.

He first learned to play tennis when he was nine, and for a few years he spent equal time playing tennis and ice hockey. However, when he was fifteen he was picked to play for his country in the Davis Cup, and he decided that from then on he would concentrate on tennis alone.

It would have been understandable if Björn, a teenager, had been intimidated by the fact that he was playing the idols of his schooldays: Ken Rosewall, Rod Laver, John Newcombe, Roy Emerson; but he is lucky in the fact that he rarely suffers from nerves before a game. This doesn't mean that he has no respect for his opponents – quite the reverse – but once he starts to play he has only one thought in his mind, and that is to win.

1976 was a good year for Björn. In the summer he won his first Wimbledon title, beating a subdued Nastase, and this only a few days after his twentieth birthday. Then, in the November, he flabbergasted the fans by announcing his engagement to a young Rumanian tennis player, Mariana Simionescu. Before this, Björn always insisted that girlfriends and tennis did not go together, but it looks as if he is prepared to risk it, and with his very real talent he shouldn't be in any danger!

Jimmy Connors

High on the favourites list of any tennis tournament is Jimmy Connors, the young American who powered his way to the top when he won the singles title at Wimbledon in 1974. That same year he was voted the best tennis player of the year, and all this at the age of 21.

After winning several major tournaments in 1975 Jimmy was hot favourite to win the Wimbledon title again, and sure enough he reached the final. However, much to everyone's surprise, his opponent, fellow American Arthur Ashe, outplayed him all the way and won the title. In spite of this defeat Jimmy continued to do well on the international circuit, playing his usual blockbusting tennis.

That powerful two-handed backhand in action, during Jimmy's match against Stan Smith.

Like many of today's young players he favours the double-handed backhand, and it is one of his most powerful shots, although he is equally strong on his forehand and backhand. He is a master of all types of surface too – grass, shale, clay, or indoor – and he has a reputation as one of the best all-rounders in the business.

Jimmy on his way to a straight sets victory over El Shafei of Egypt.

Jimmy is always popular with the spectators, not only because he plays good tennis but also because he keeps his sense of humour during a game and can laugh at his mistakes. This rapport with the crowd was very evident during his successful doubles partnership with Ilie Nastase, and their light-hearted antics brought some fun back into the game.

For a time, Jimmy was engaged to another superstar of the tennis world, Chrissy Evert, but that seems to have ended now. All in all he's quite a popular guy, whether on or off the court!

SUE BARKER

Sue Barker on her way to a 6–4, 7–5 victory over C. Martinez of America.

Hailed as our brightest hope for the future, Sue Barker is poised to take over Virginia Wade's number 1 spot in British tennis. Sue, a pretty blonde from Devon, is a relative newcomer to international tennis, but already she has beaten some of the world's best and she is improving all the time.

Her strongest stroke is her forehand, but she is a good all rounder, and has the calm temperament to see her through a tense match. She is a fighter too, and has often come back after losing the first set to win the match.

In November 1976 she was picked for the Wightman Cup team, and although Great Britain lost to the United States, Sue played well and took the world's number 1, Chrissy Evert, to three sets. She was pleased with her performance, and felt that international competition of this kind was what she needed to polish up her game.

Great Britain has not had a Wimbledon champion since Ann Jones beat Billy Jean King in the late 1960s, but who knows, we may have a future champion in Sue. Let's hope so!

NO KIDDING!

One of the most successful acts ever to be launched on the TV talent show 'New Faces' was the Liverpool vocal group, Our Kid, seen here looking pretty pleased with themselves!

The song they sang on New Faces, *You Just Might See Me Cry* – which was soon to be a hit single – notched up a remarkable 118 marks, out of a possible 120. And the viewers' panel, sometimes at variance with the judges, also had no hesitation in voting Our Kid outright winners of the show.

They're not strictly Superstars yet, you might be saying, but one thing's sure: the future certainly looks bright for this talented young foursome. No kidding!

KEEPING UP WITH CAT STEVENS

Cat Stevens has come a long way since the days of *Morning Has Broken* and *Moonshadow.* Always a sensitive writer, his work has the added depth and maturity that makes classic music, and although he has moved away from the old 'pop' image, he is more popular than ever. He tours all over the world, and his concerts are always a sell-out.

One thing that hasn't changed though is Cat's use of unusual rhythms and phrasing. No matter what the mood of the song, he gives it that distinctive stamp that makes all his music so memorable. His ballads are simple and direct, but they are songs that people can identify with. His up-tempo numbers are cheerful, catchy and optimistic.

Cat's artistic talents are still well to the fore too. After his charming cover designs for the albums *Tea for the Tillerman* and *Teaser and the Firecat,* he wrote and illustrated a delightful story to accompany his *Numbers* album, which was released at the end of 1975. Singer, songwriter, artist, musician: most people would be content to be just one, but Cat Stevens combines them all, and that's what makes him a superstar!

Bryan Ferry

Whatever else Bryan Ferry may have, he certainly has style. Equally at home on stage at a rock concert, or on the pages of a glossy magazine, he is as distinctive as diamonds, as classy as caviare.

When other bands wore jeans and T-shirts, he wore white dinner jackets and bow ties. When they wore long hair, he slicked his back and wore a pencil-thin moustache. His tremulous, doom-laden voice is like nothing you have ever heard, and yet he can belt out rock numbers with Roxy Music, or croon over the moody ballads of the fifties with equal success. He is constantly in the charts, both with Roxy and on his own, and whatever the song, he brings to it his own, highly individual style.

Much of this distinctive character is due to the fact that, before he got into music, Bryan was an artist. After studying at the Royal College of Art he painted and worked in ceramics, and it wasn't until 1970 that he decided to teach himself to play the piano. He wrote a dozen songs too, and by the end of the year he had formed Roxy Music. This wasn't his first musical venture; during the sixties he sang with a band called Gas Board, but at that time painting was still his first love.

Now he divides his time between his work with the band and his solo career, and although the two styles are quite different, one thing is sure: the Bryan Ferry style will never change!

Dennis Waterman

Can you imagine a musical version of *The Sweeney . . .* With Regan doing the old soft shoe and Carter providing the vocals? Not as far-fetched as you might think, now that Dennis Waterman has started a recording career, although, come to think of it, Regan *might* draw the line at the dancing!

Look out for Dennis in the full length, *non*-musical feature film of *The Sweeney,* and also for his album, *Down Wind of Angels.*

Bob Dylan, poet and folk-singer, was born in Duluth, Minnesota, in 1941. When he was twelve he decided to learn the guitar and was the instigator of several groups at High School.

He entered the University of Minnesota in 1959 but was soon heading for Greenwich Village where, as a drop-out, he then sang professionally.

His style from the first has been unique. Earthy, disturbing, sensitive, probing – you name it, his songs speak.

Dylan, along with his rivals The Beatles, developed Rock in the '60s, but his ability to communicate is such that we can say, without a doubt, that he's shaken up the consciousness of audiences and quiet listeners to his discs, in many

BOB DYLAN

parts of the world.

Bob Dylan (Robert Zimmerman's his real name) signed a contract with CBS in 1962 and his first album was sensational. He has toured Britain several times – with mixed receptions.

The quiet revolution goes on, and instigators through history have never had it easy! Let's hope that Dylan will continue to have his say for many years to come.

Discs, still in circulation:
Bob Dylan (CBS 1962); John Wesley Harding (CBS 1968); Greatest Hits (CBS 1967). Planet Waves (Asylum 1974); Before The Flood (Asylum double 1974); While The Establishment Burns; Royal Albert Hall 1966; Black Nite Crash; 40 Red White And Blue Shoestrings.